# This Awesome Bird Coloring Book



# belongs to

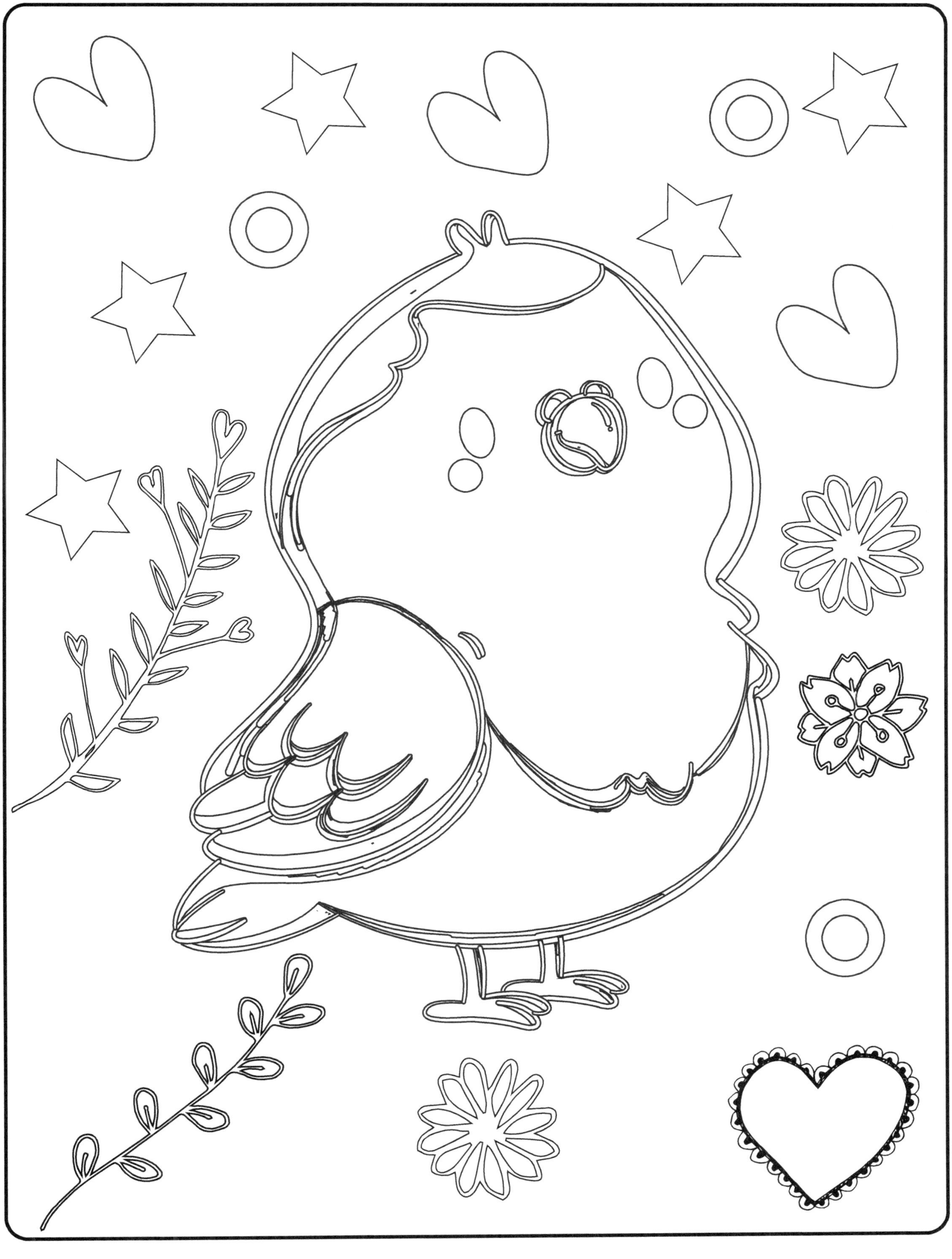

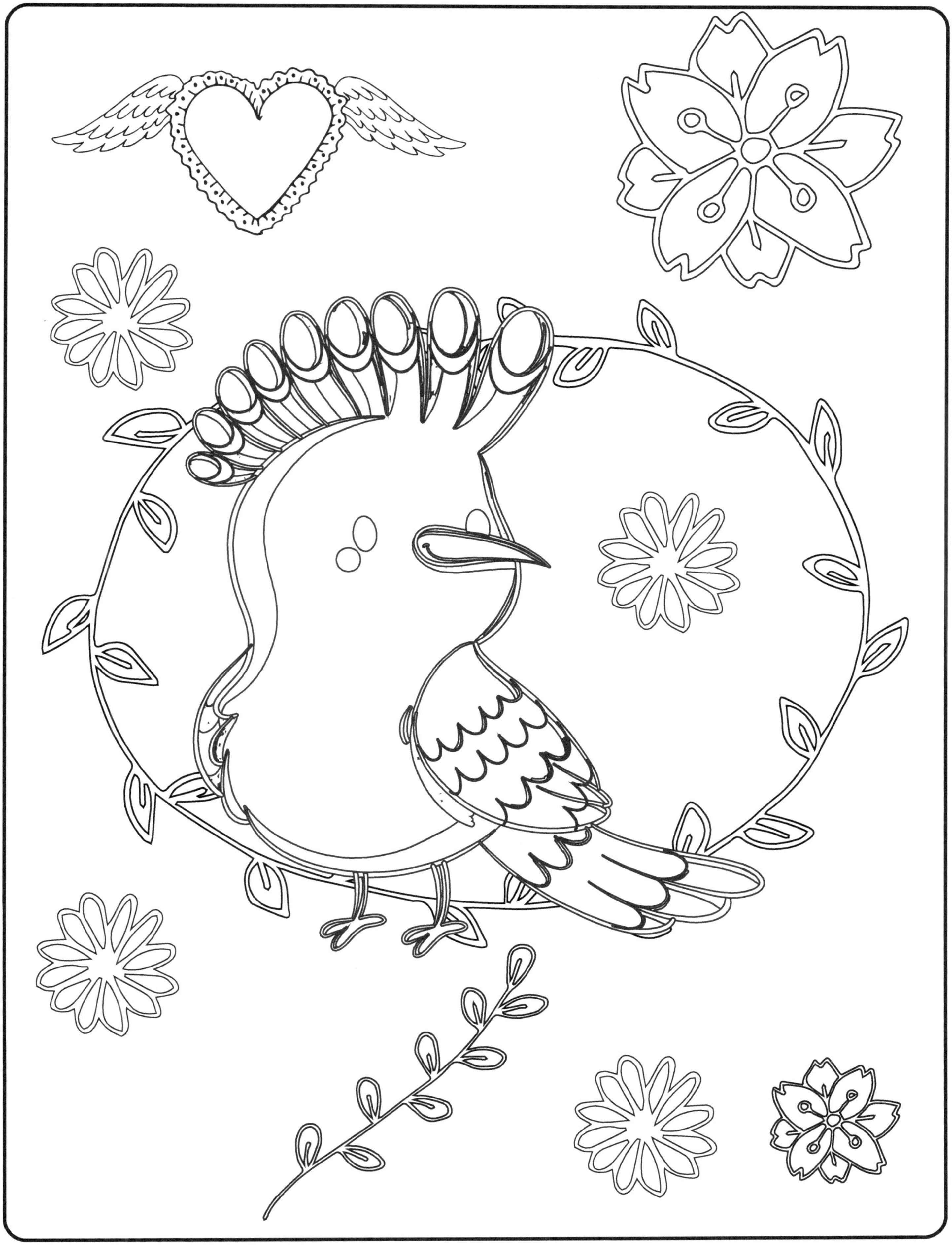

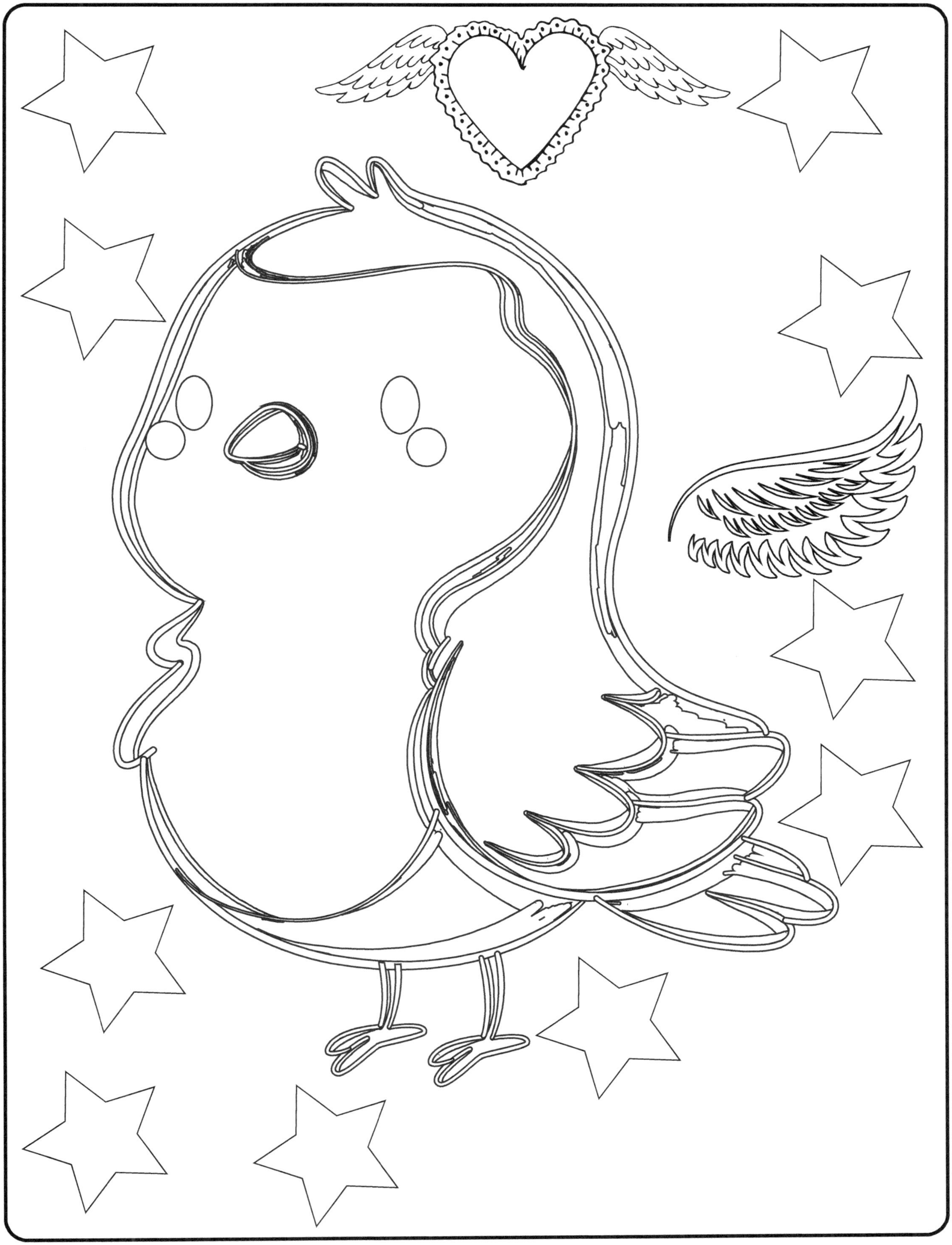

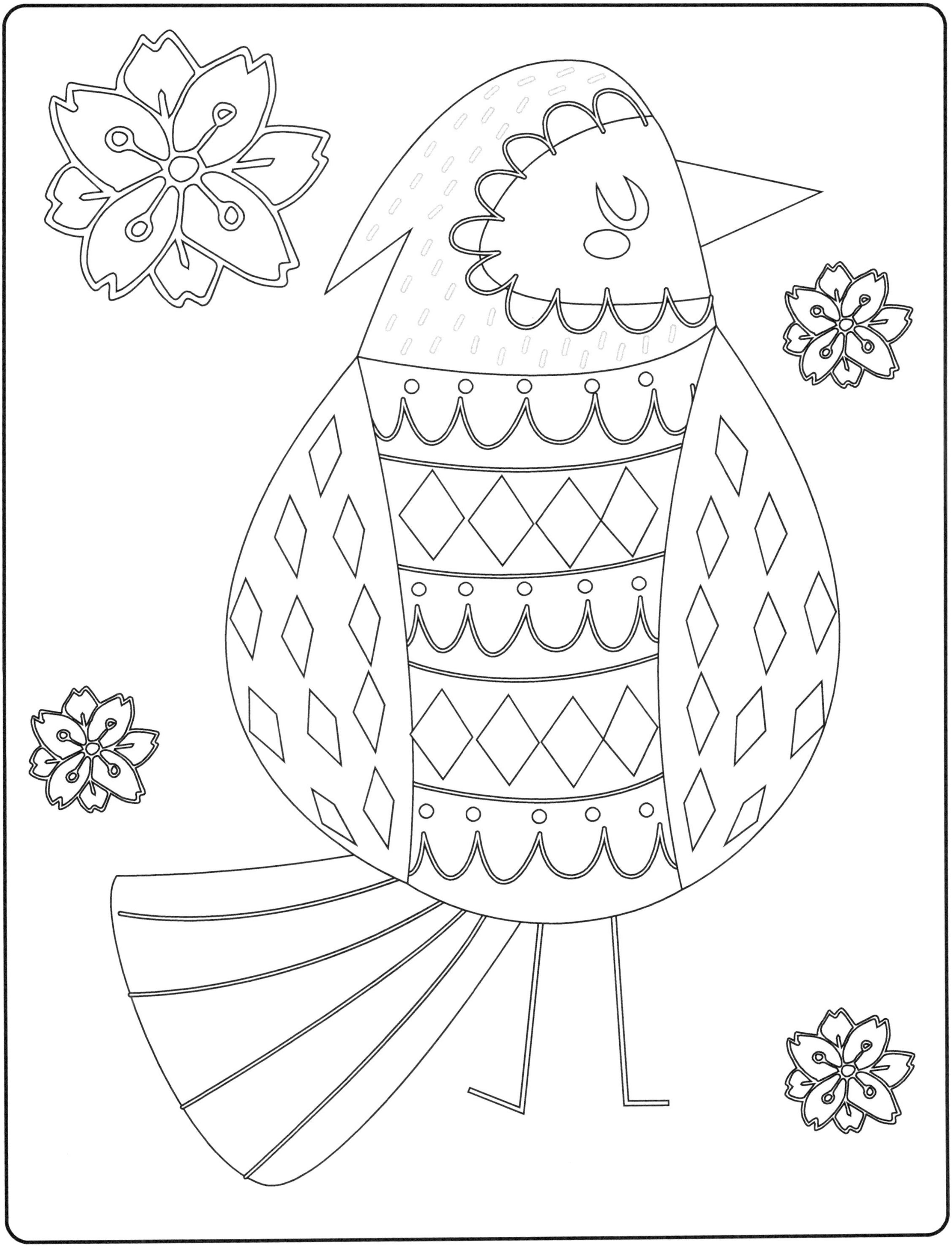

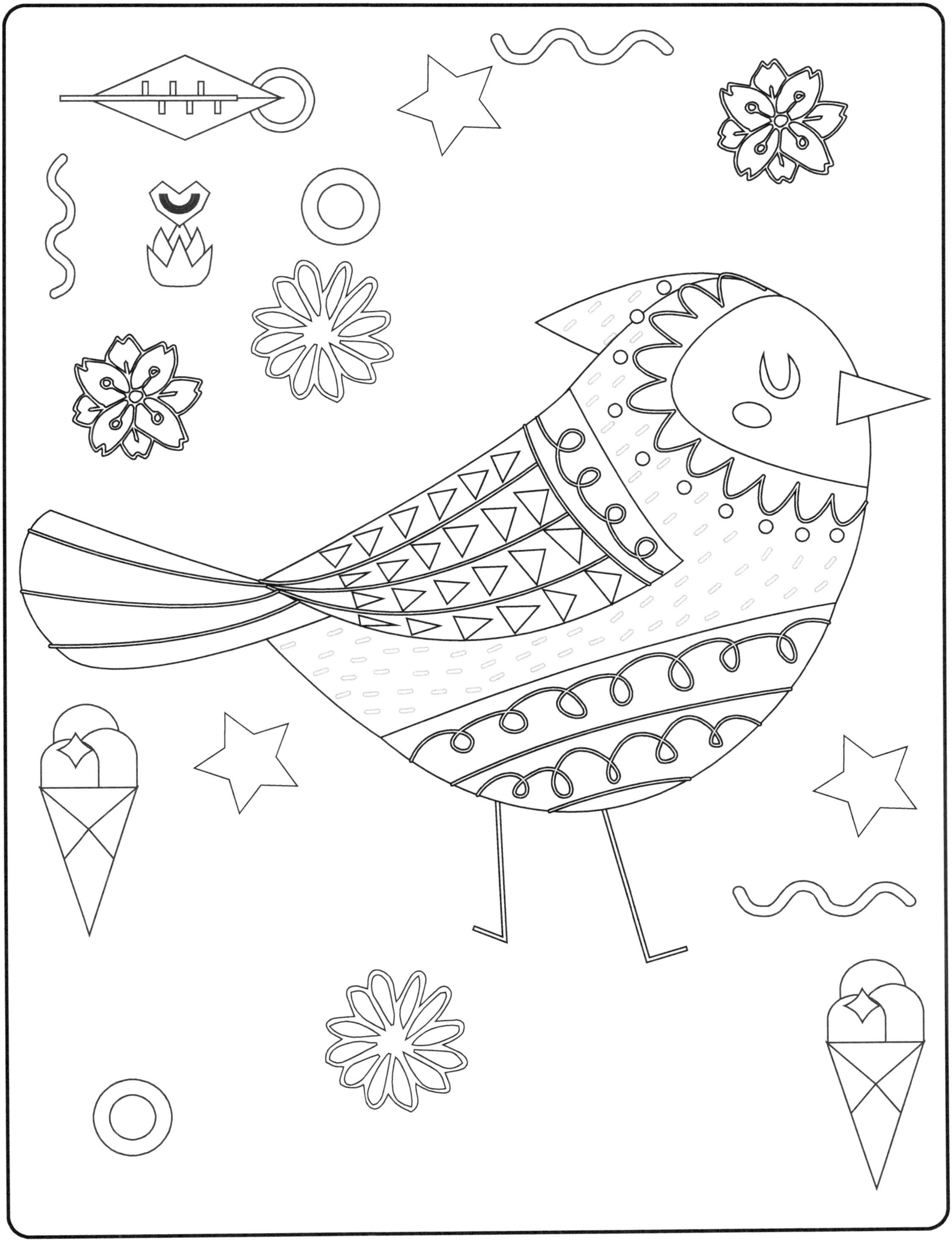

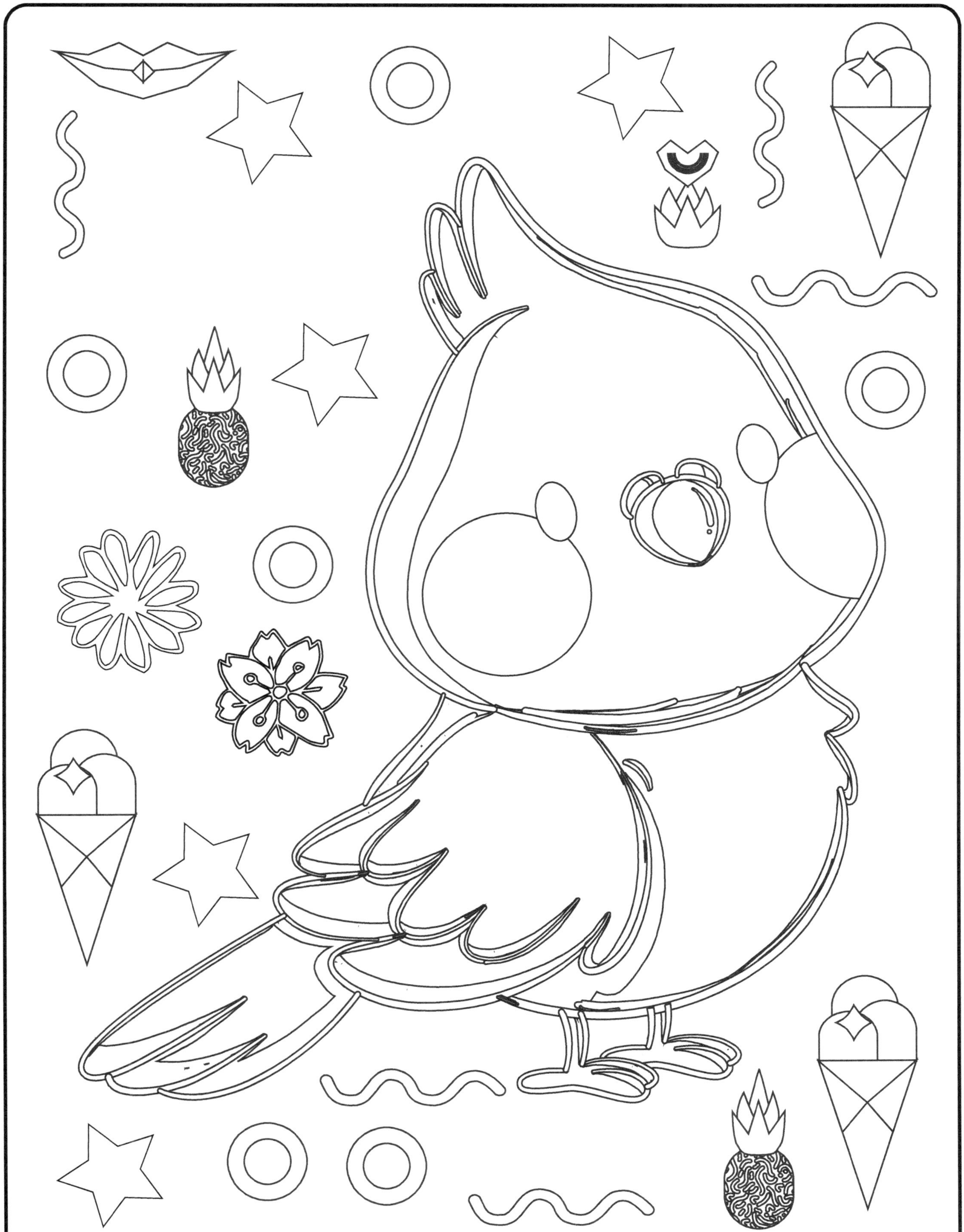

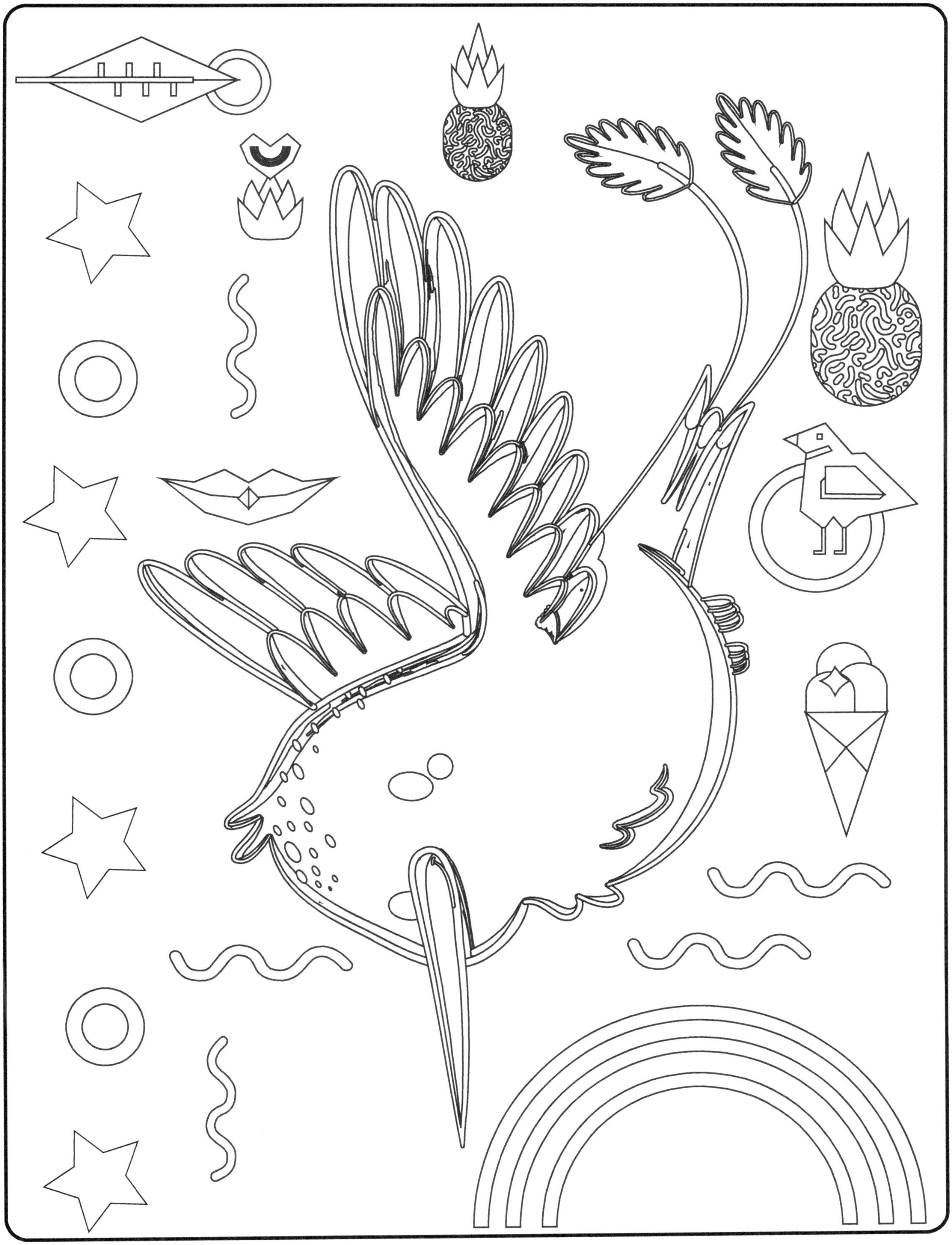

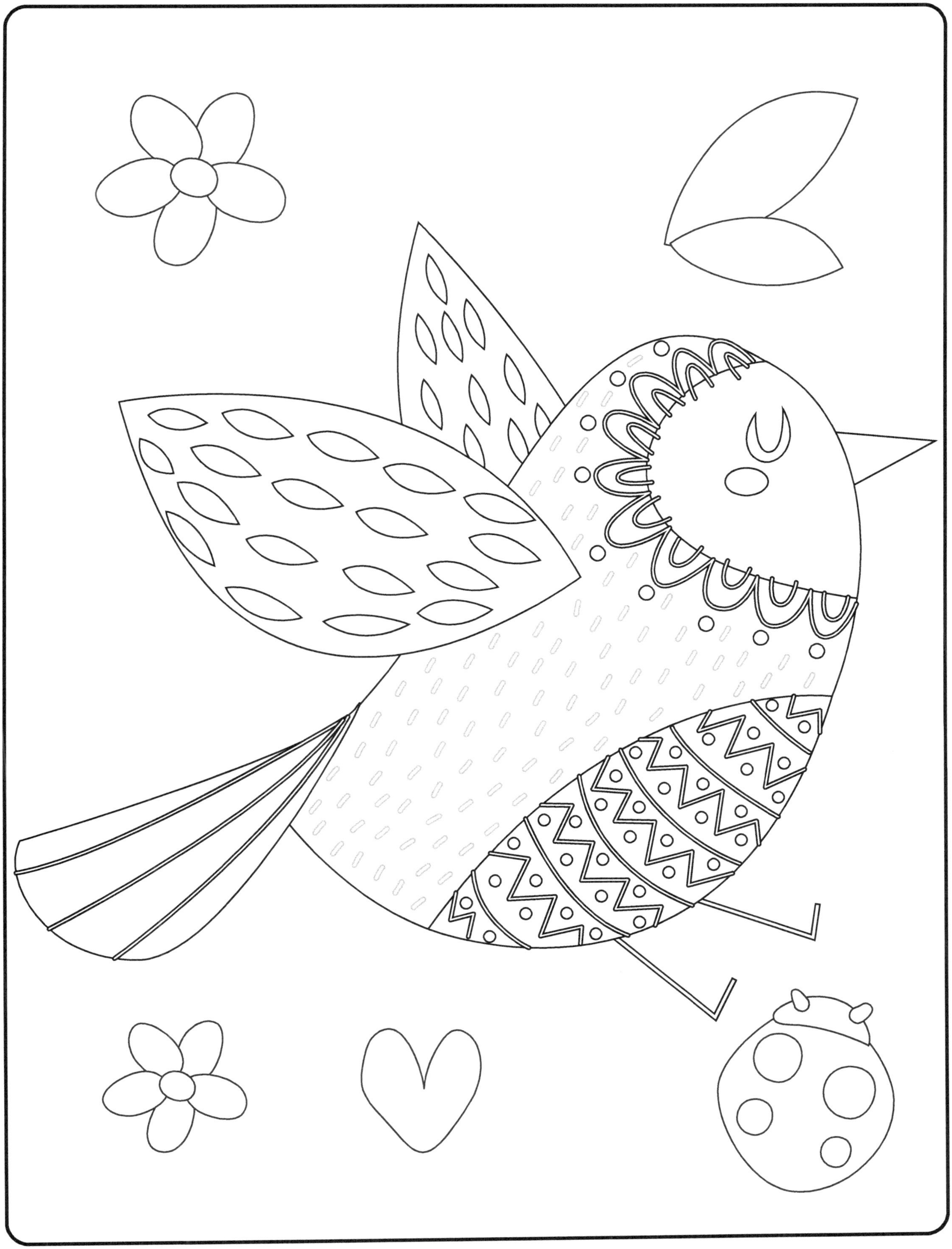

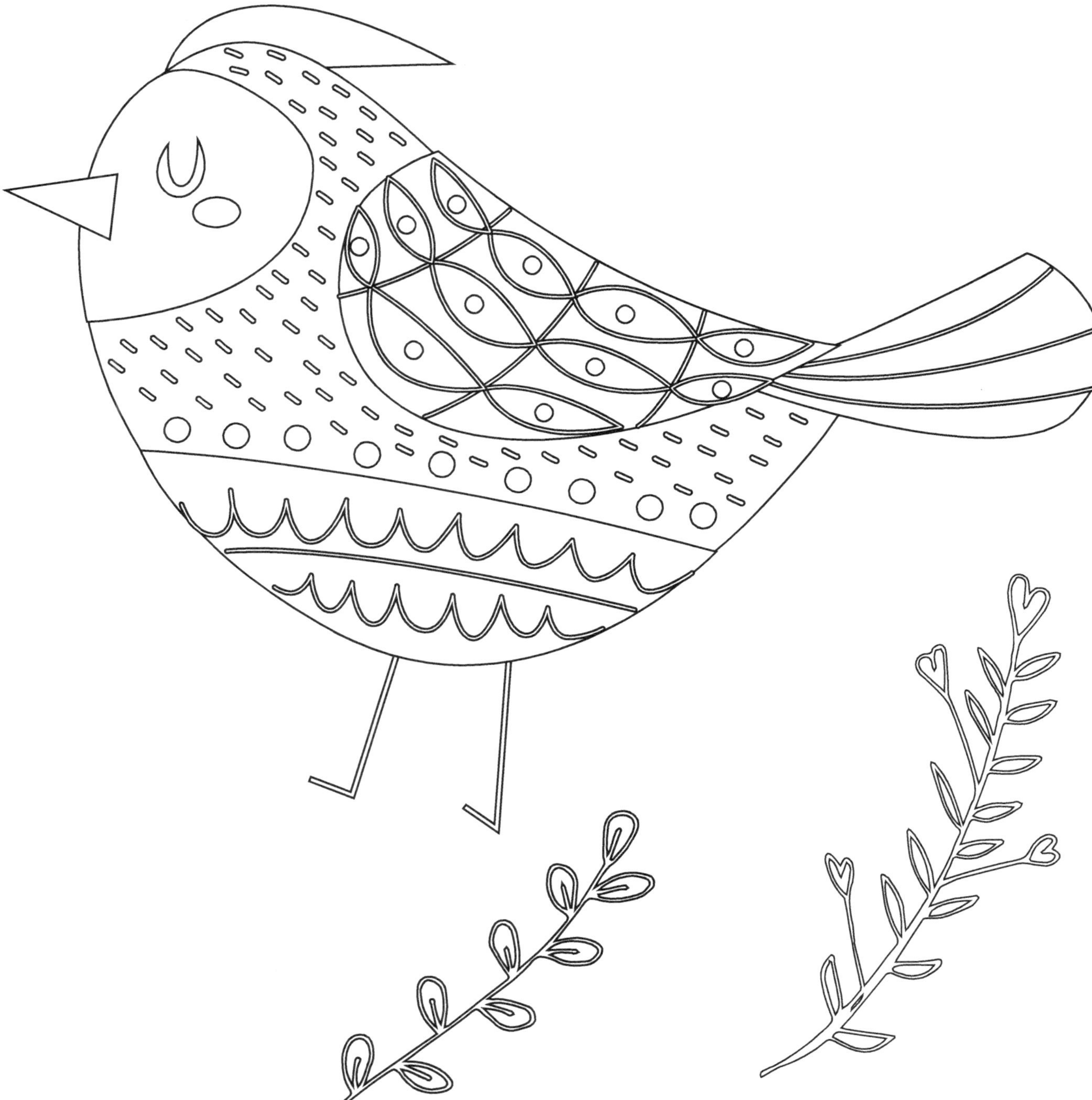

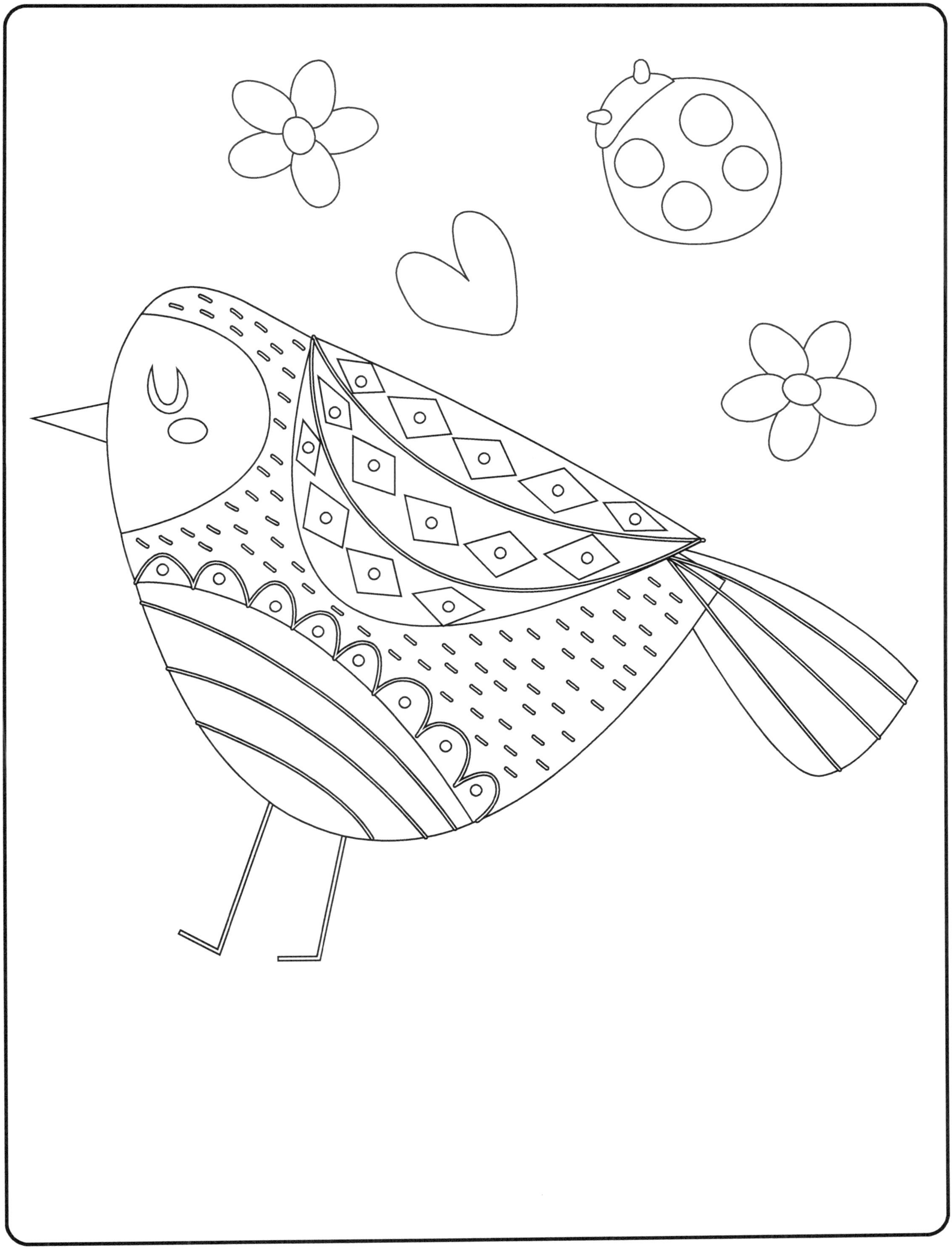

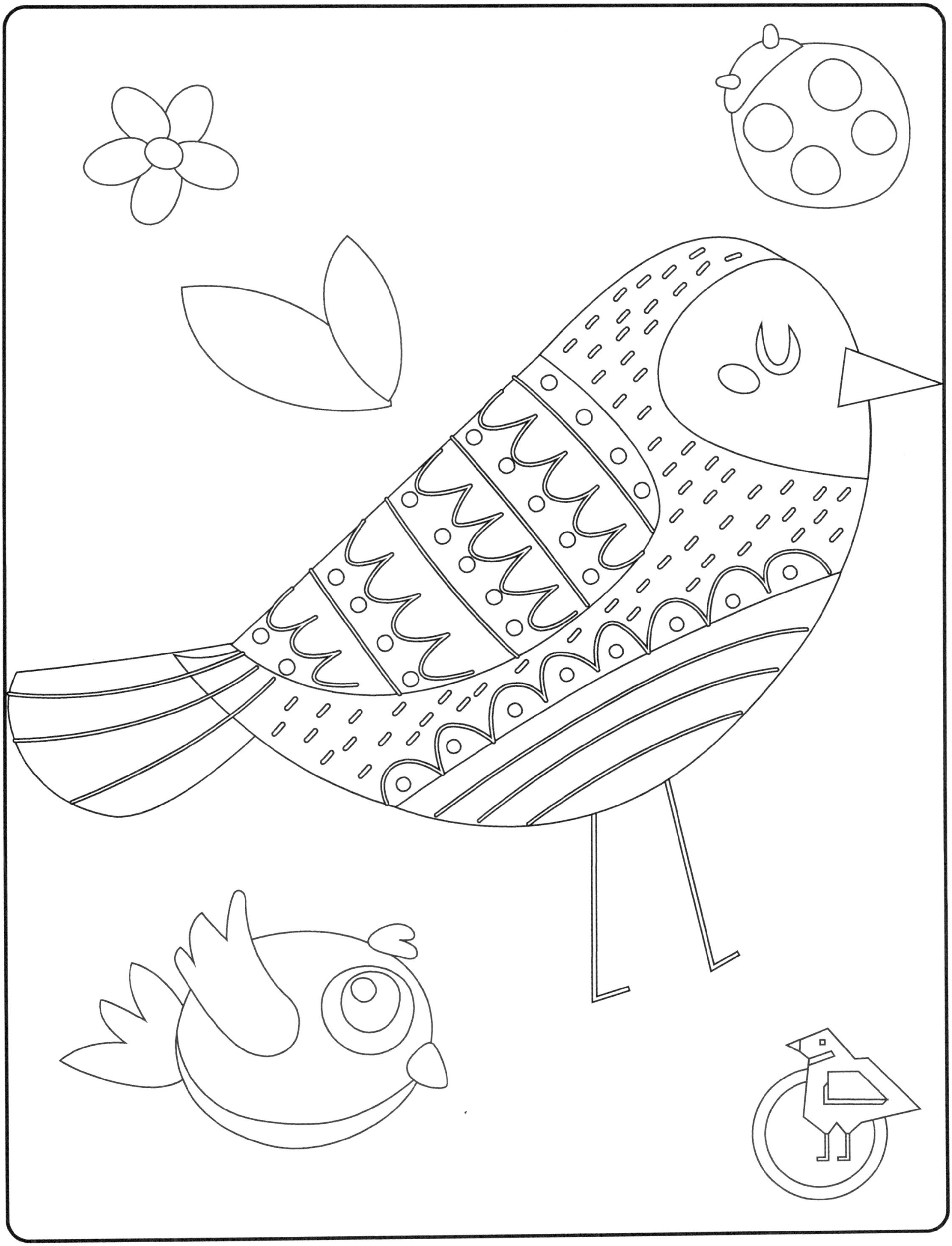

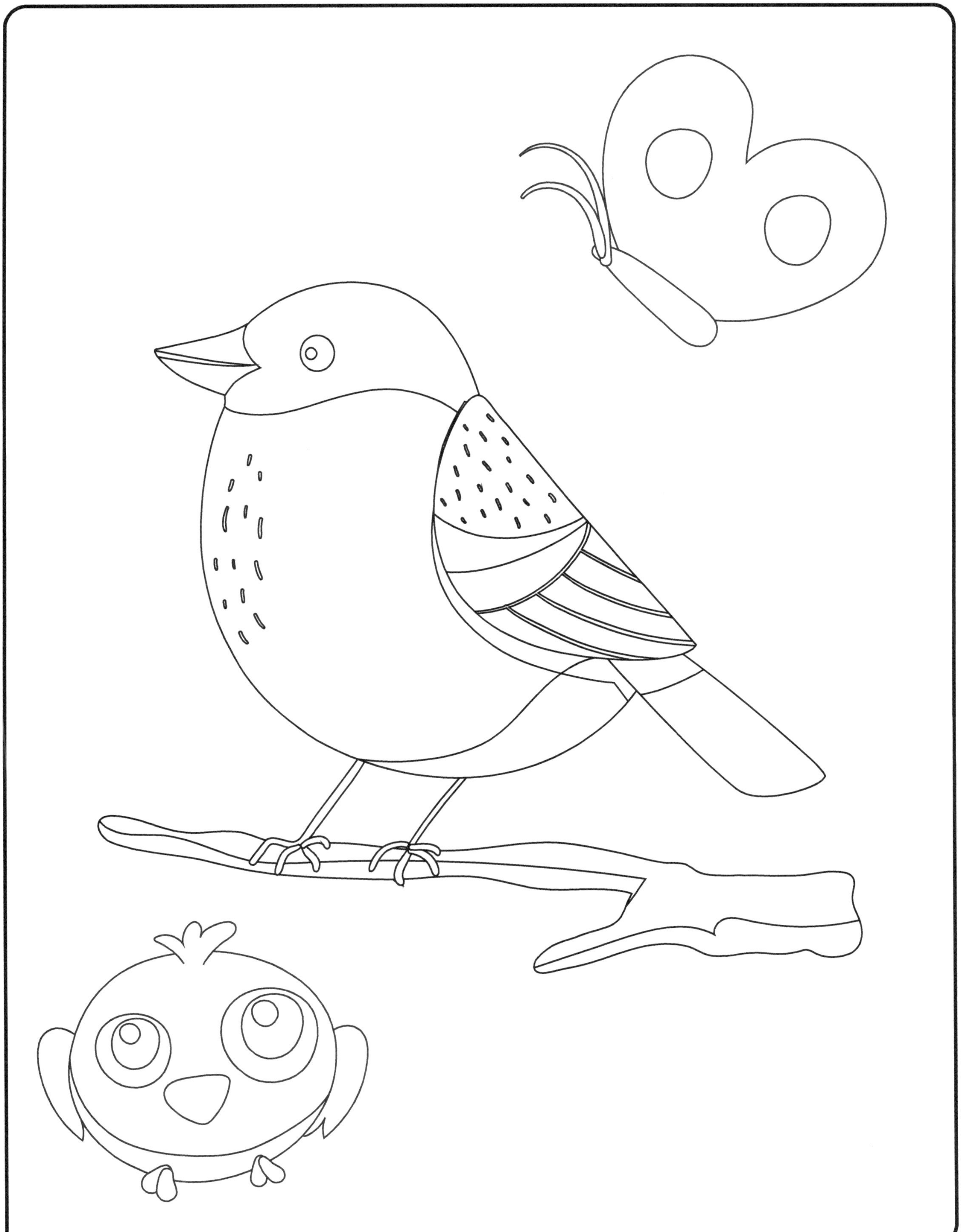

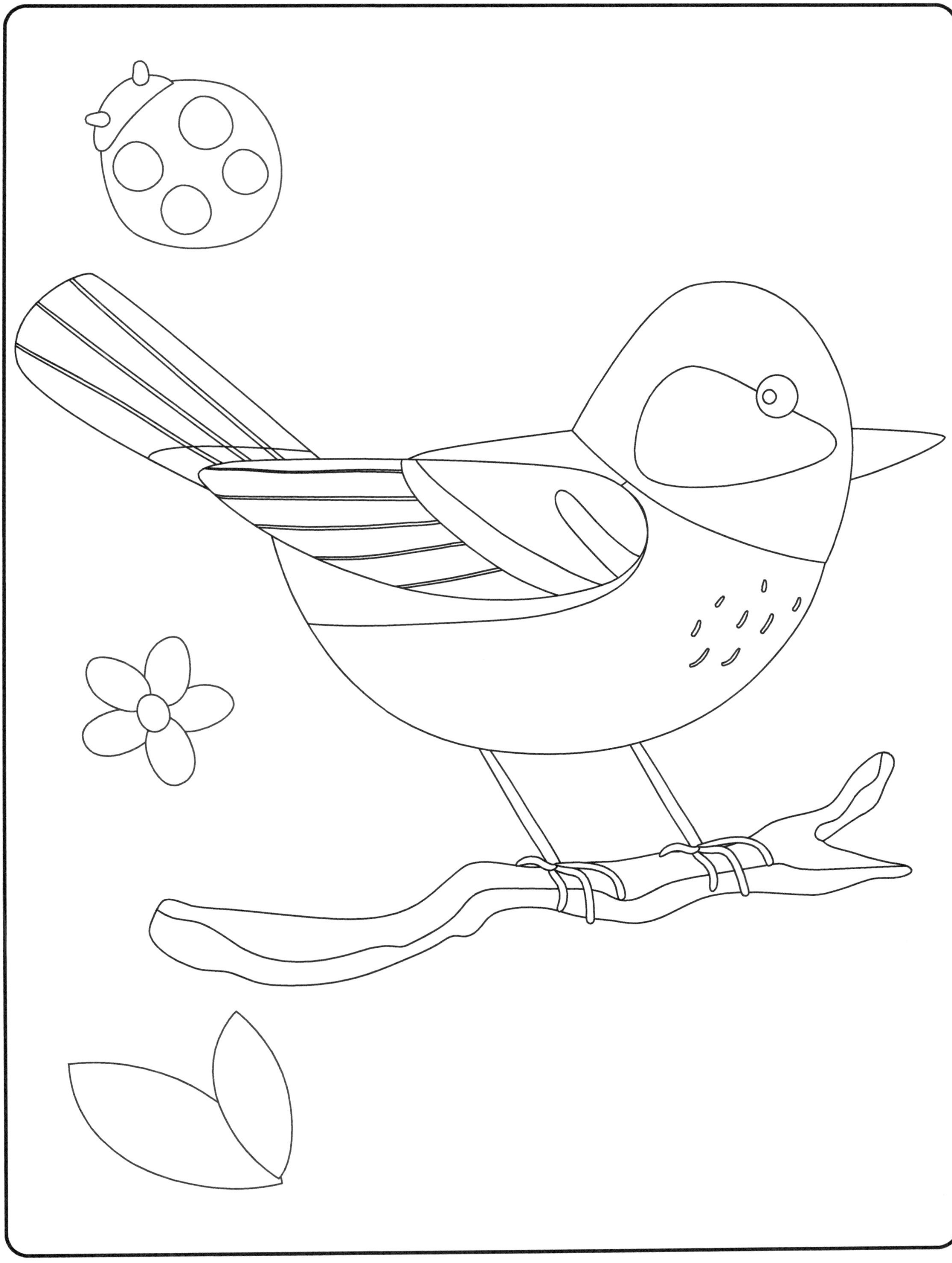

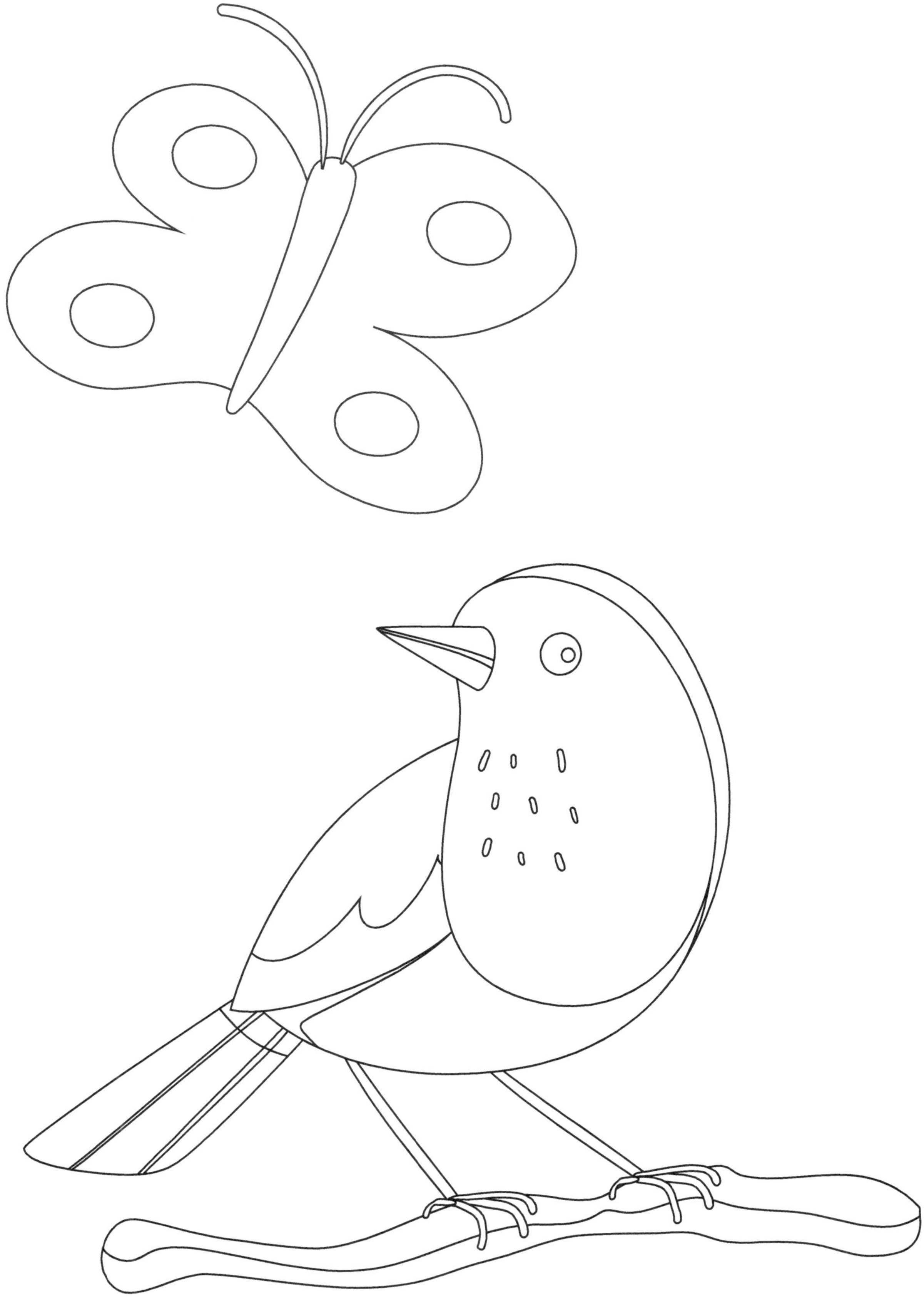

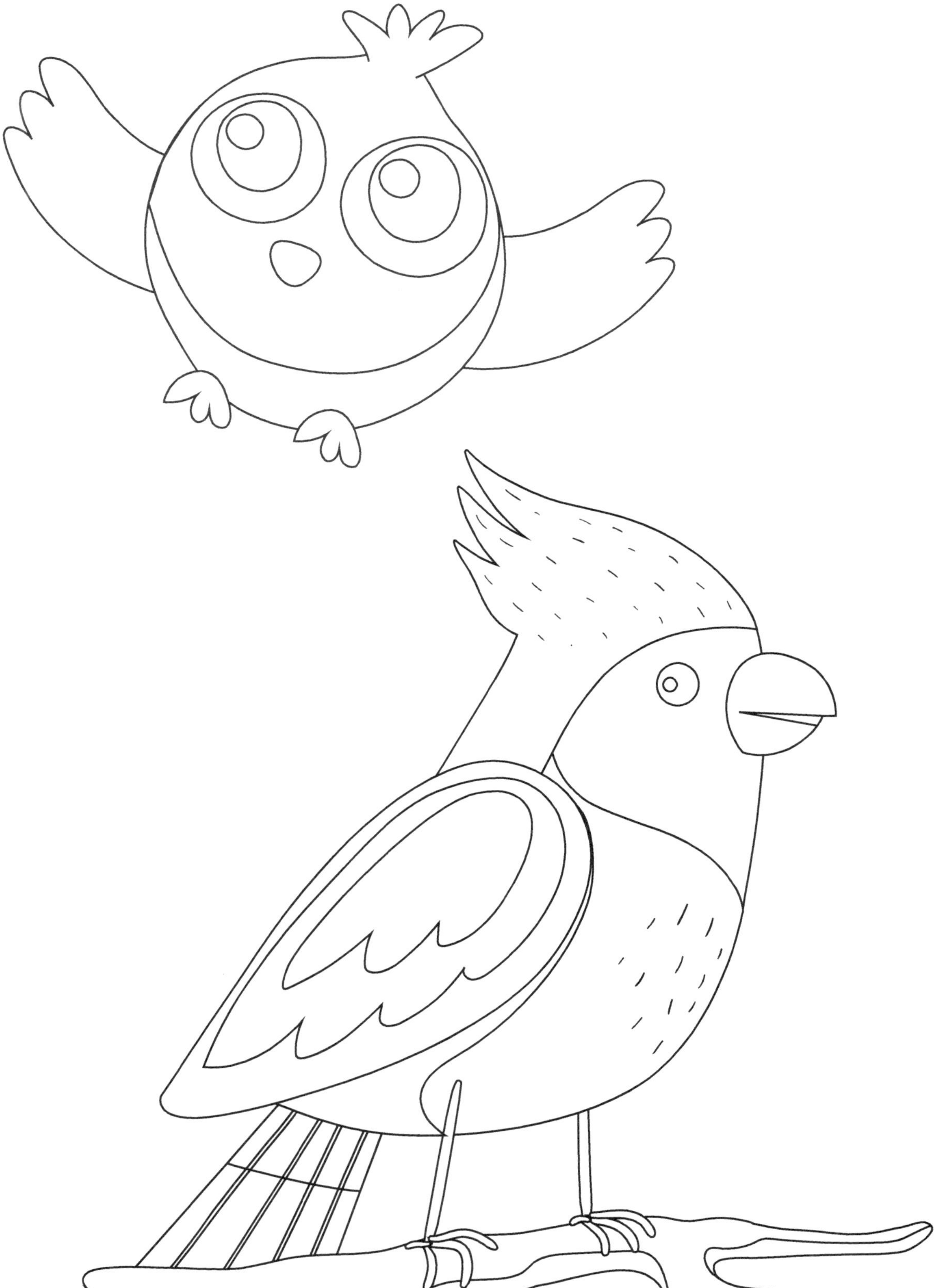

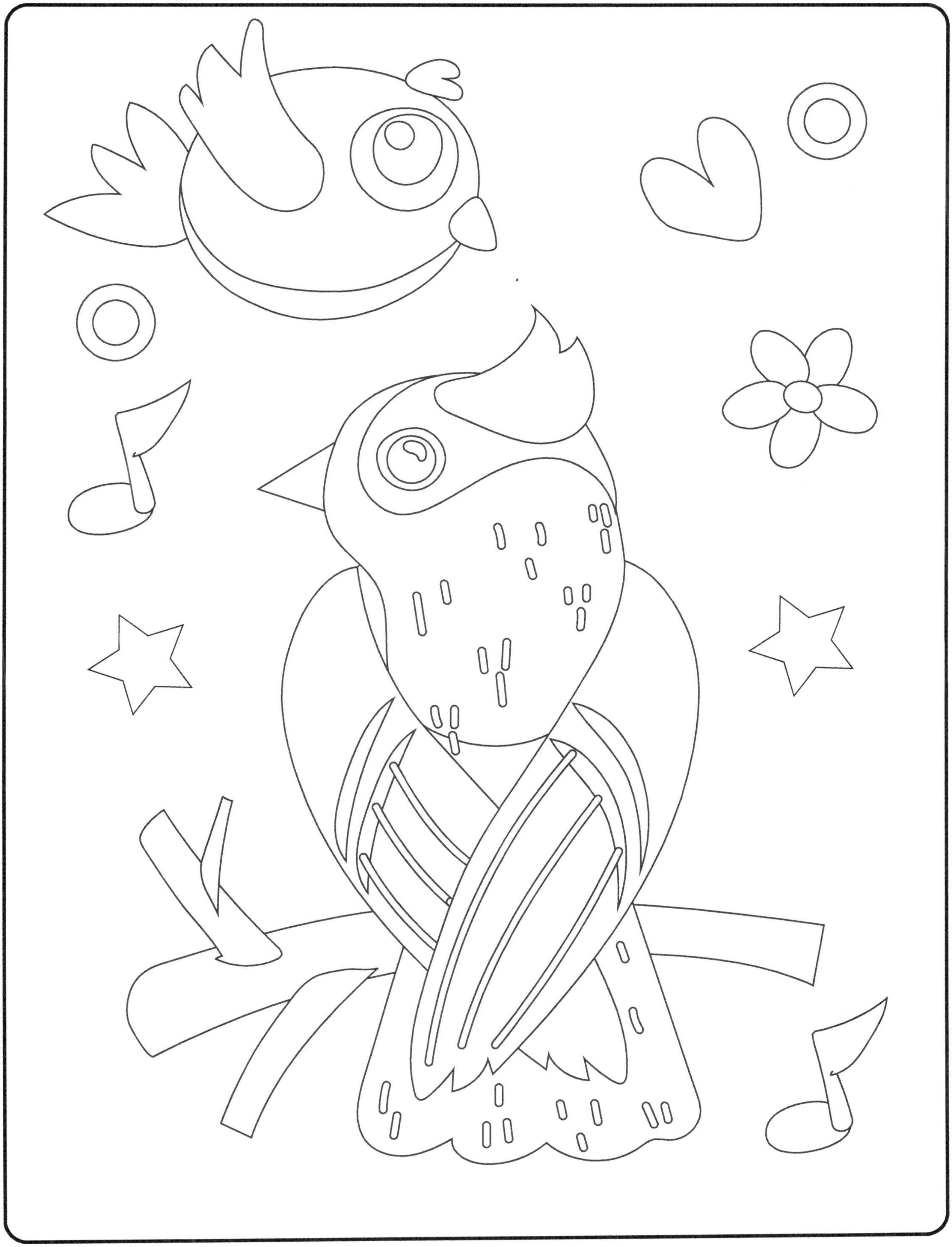

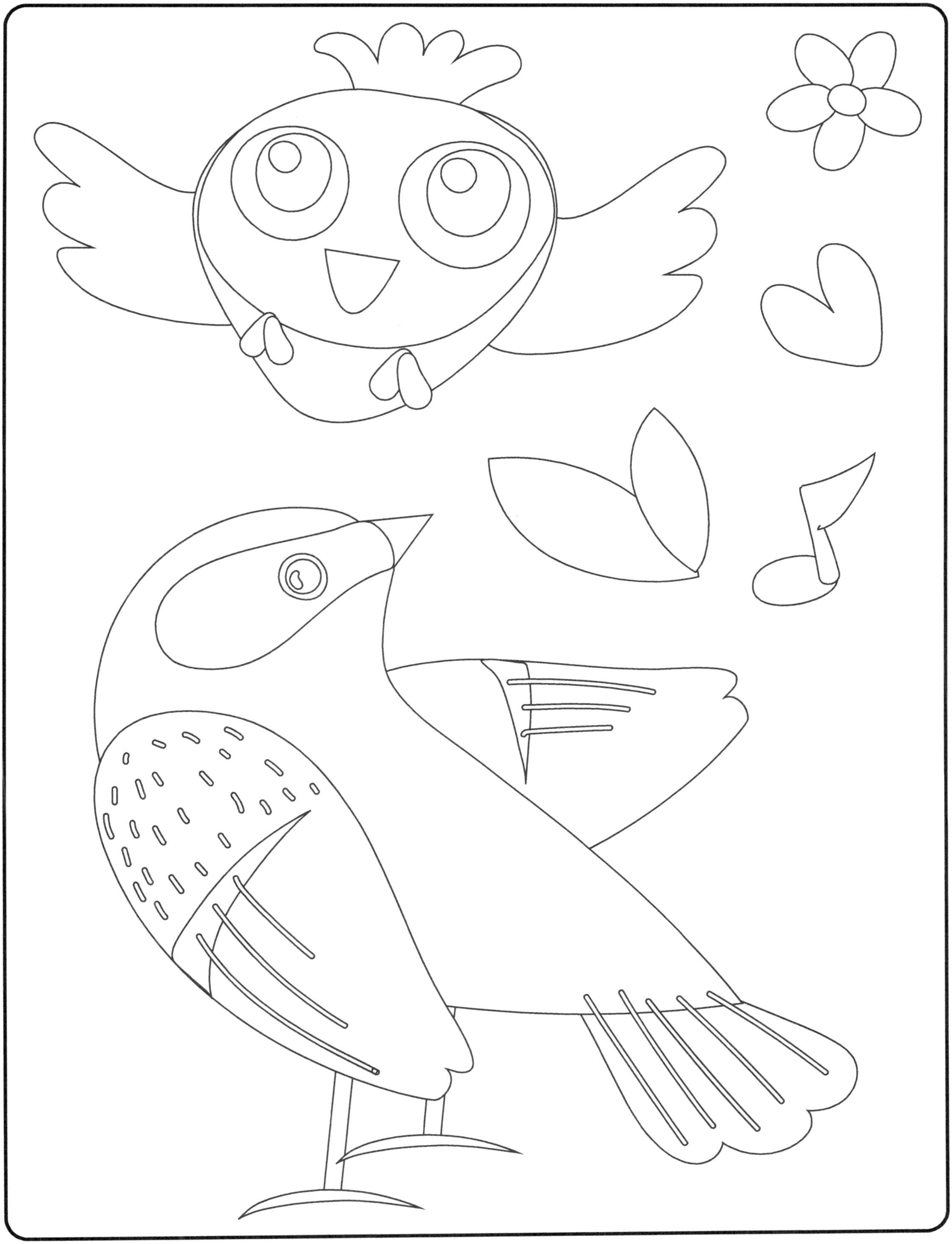

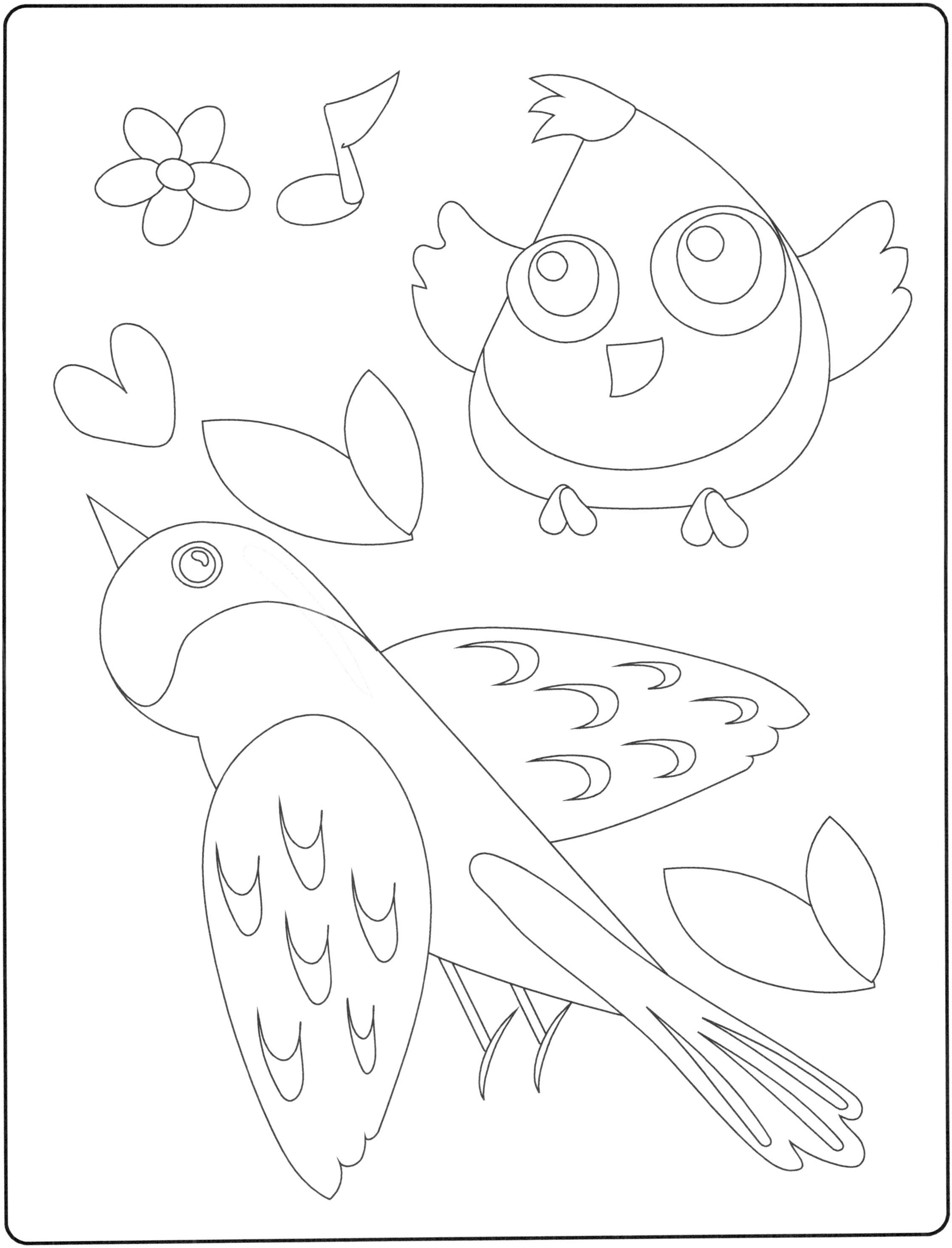

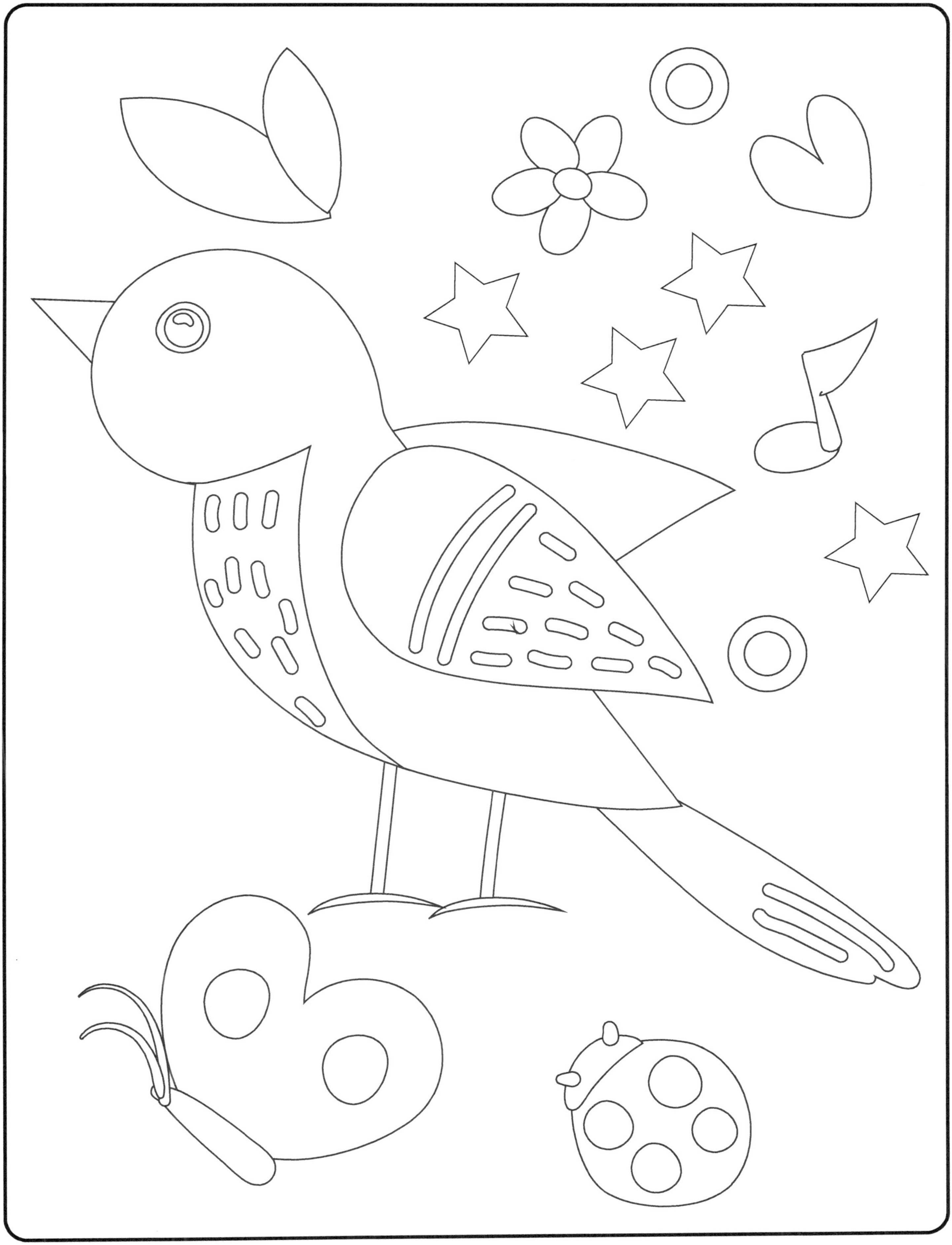

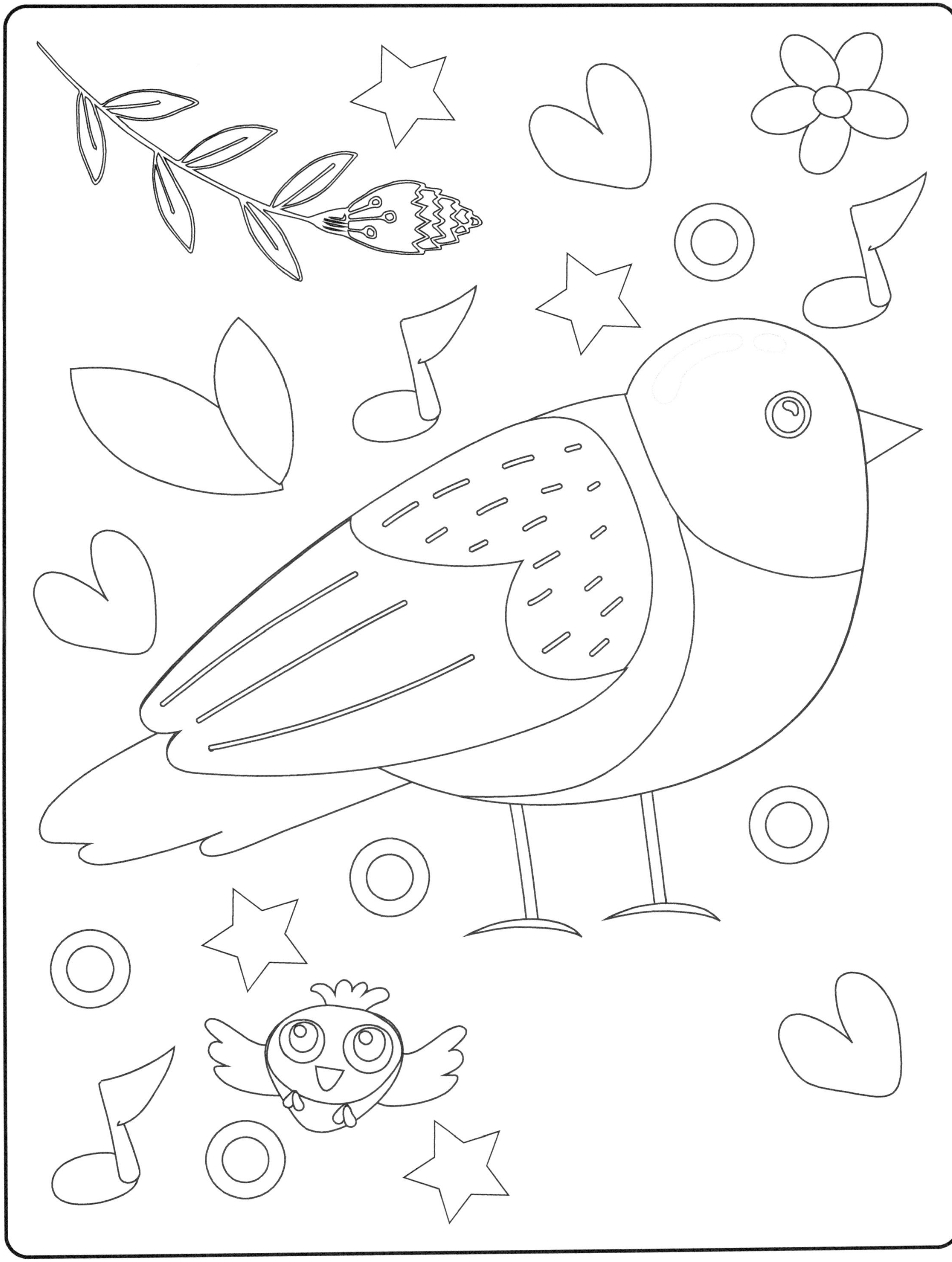

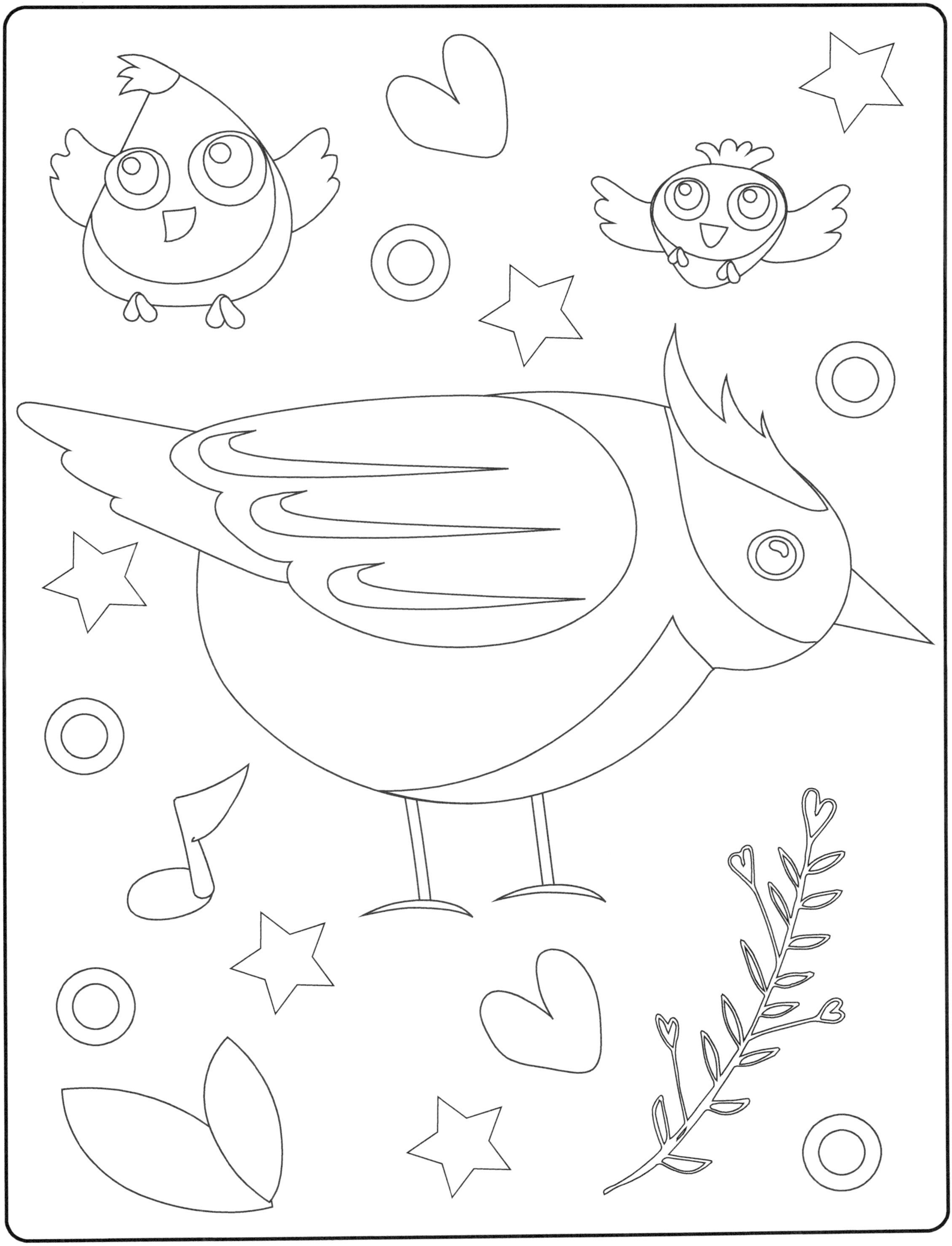

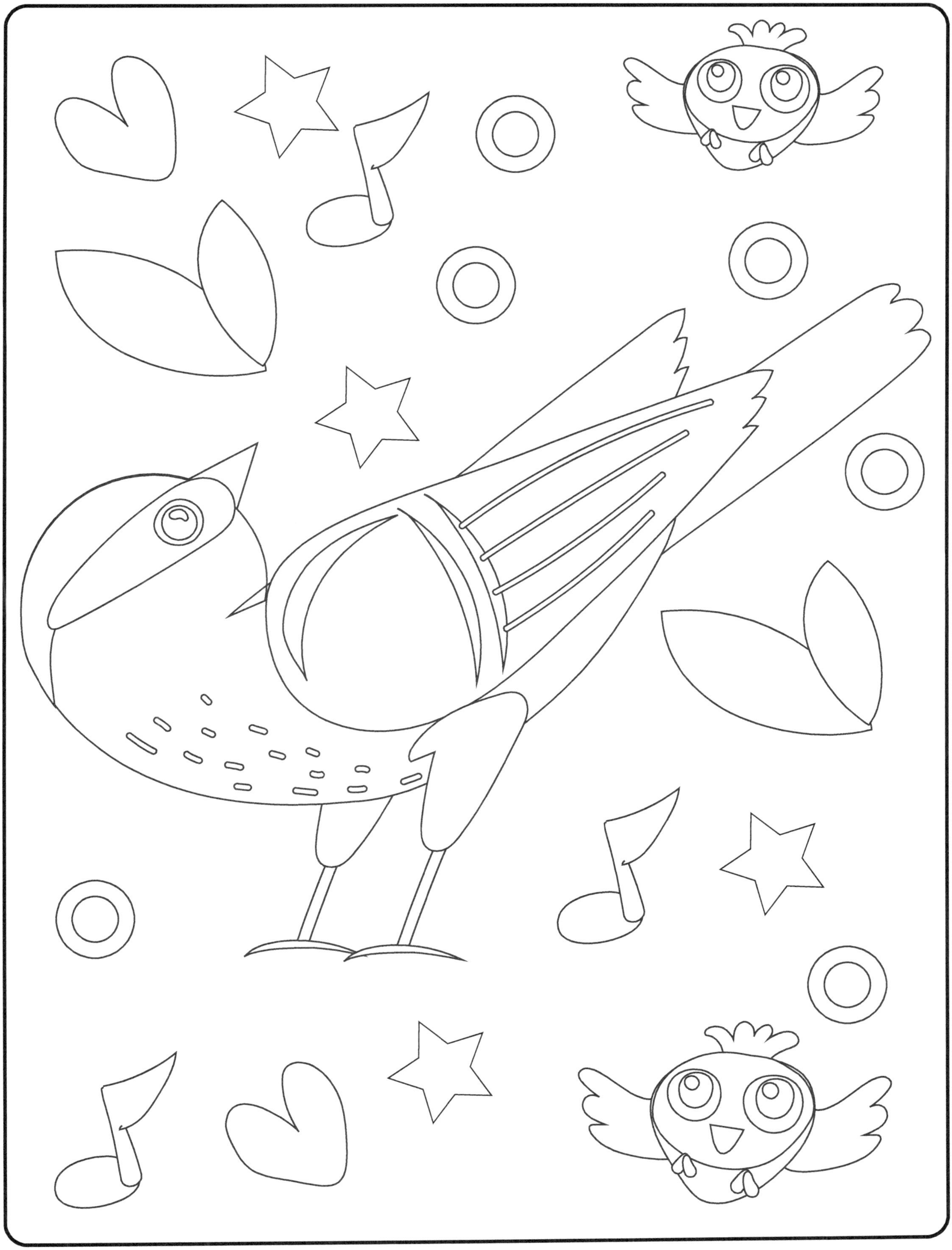

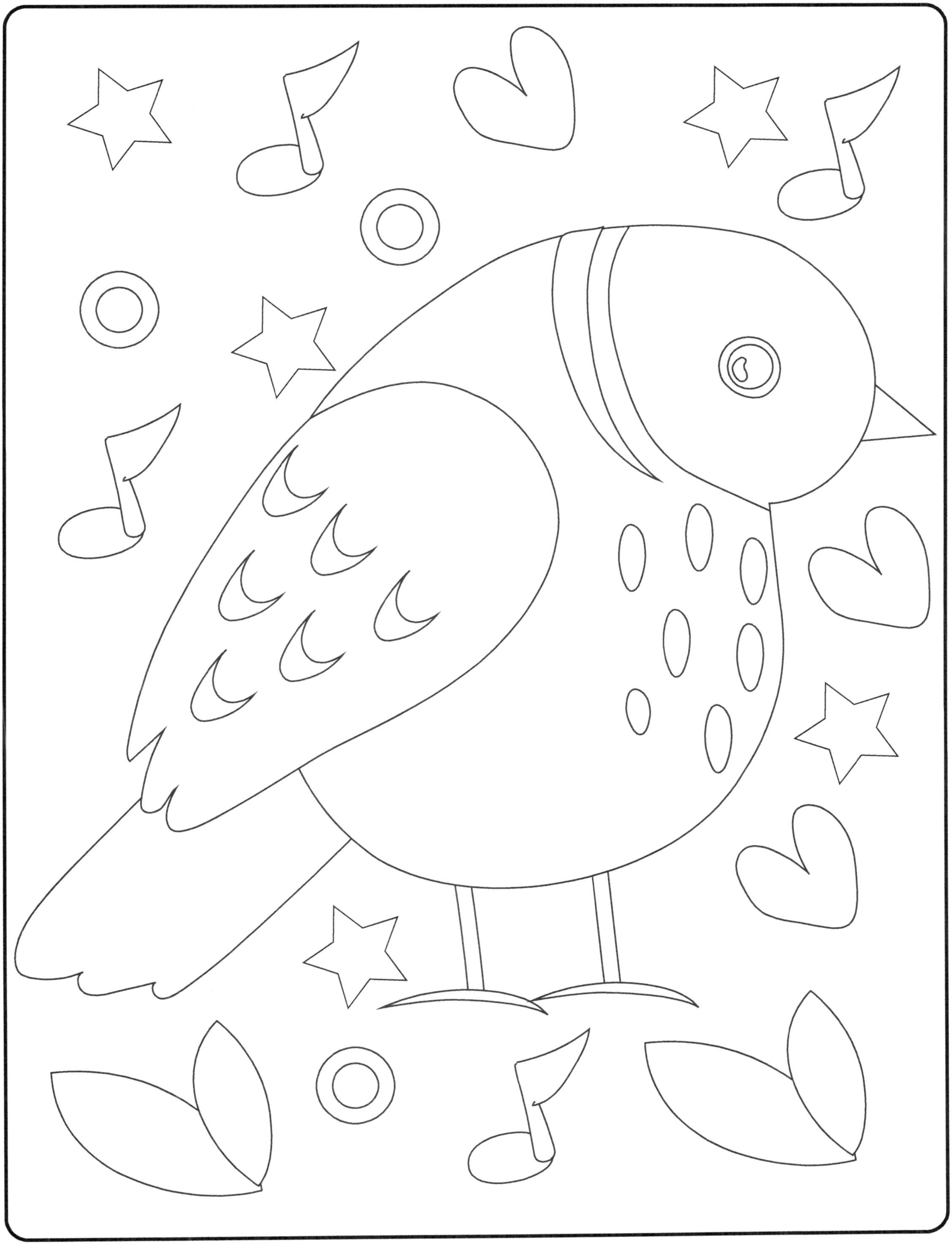

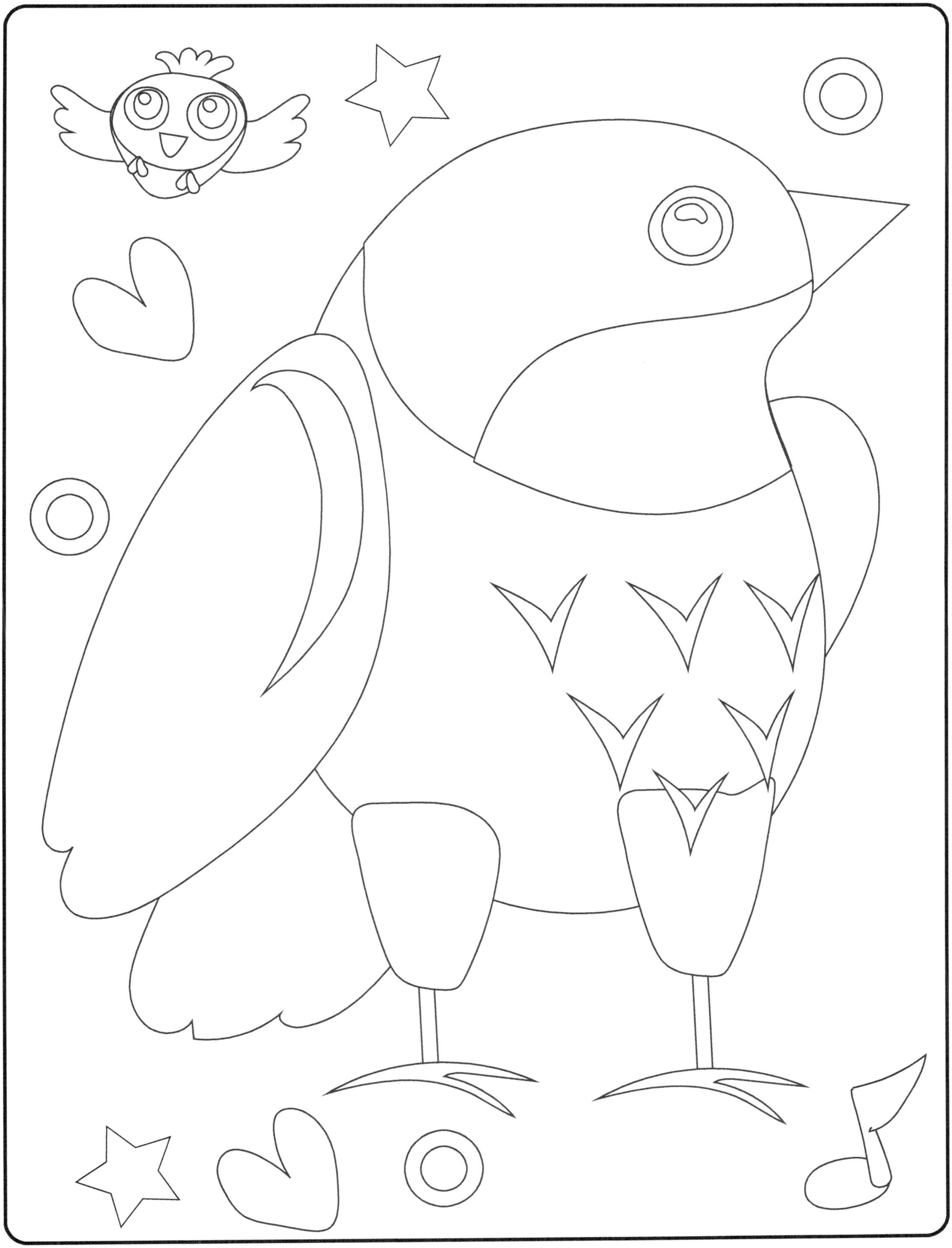

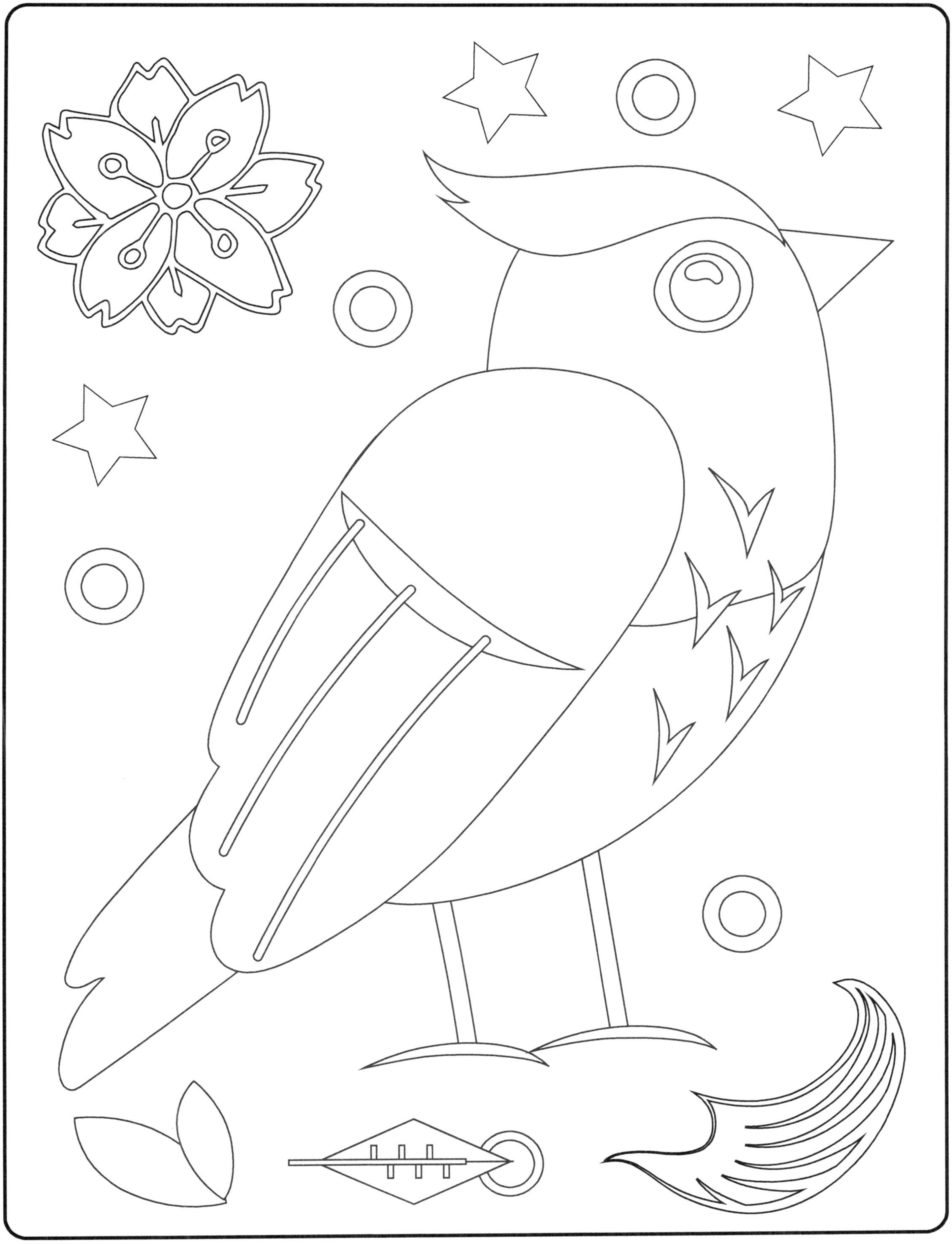

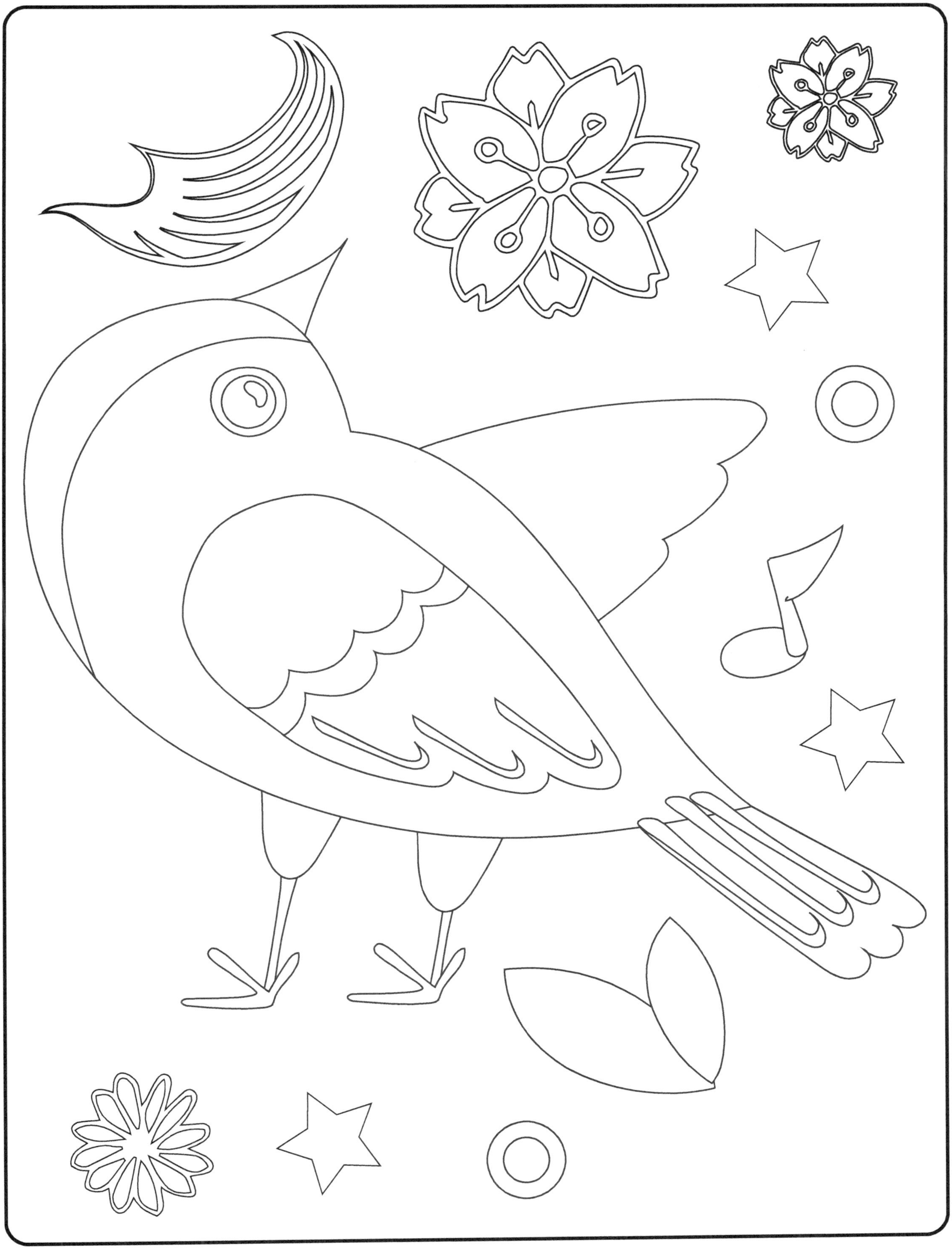

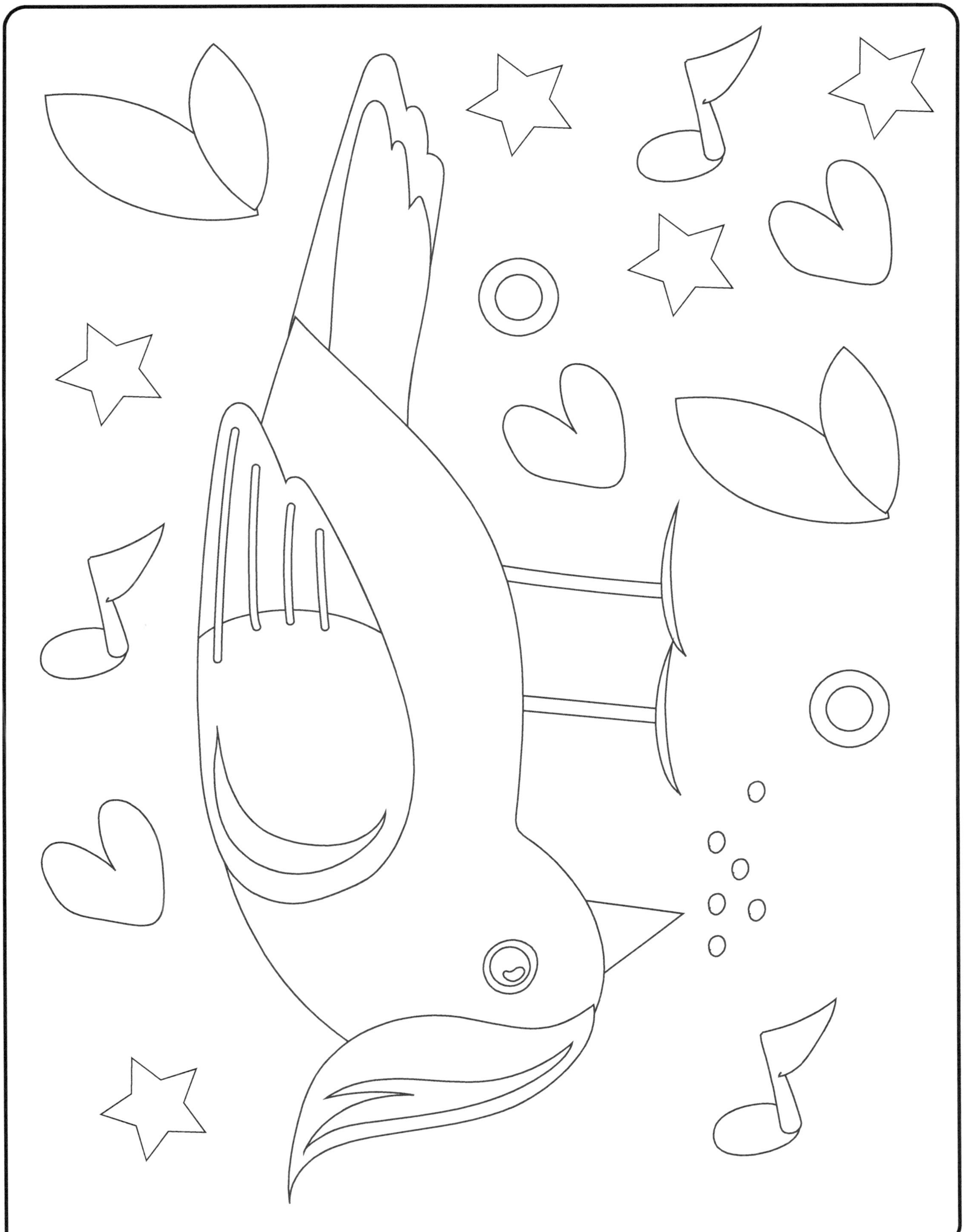

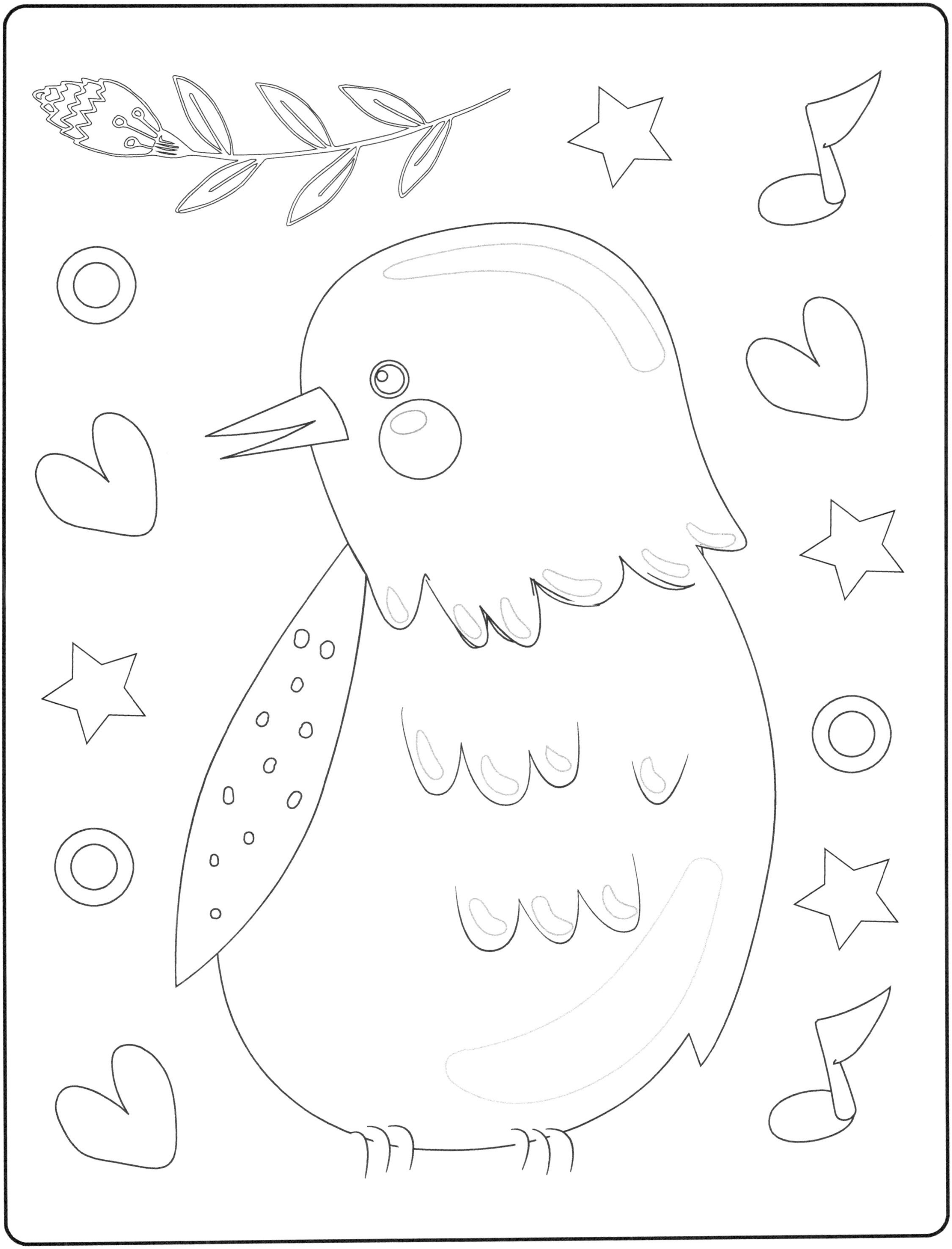

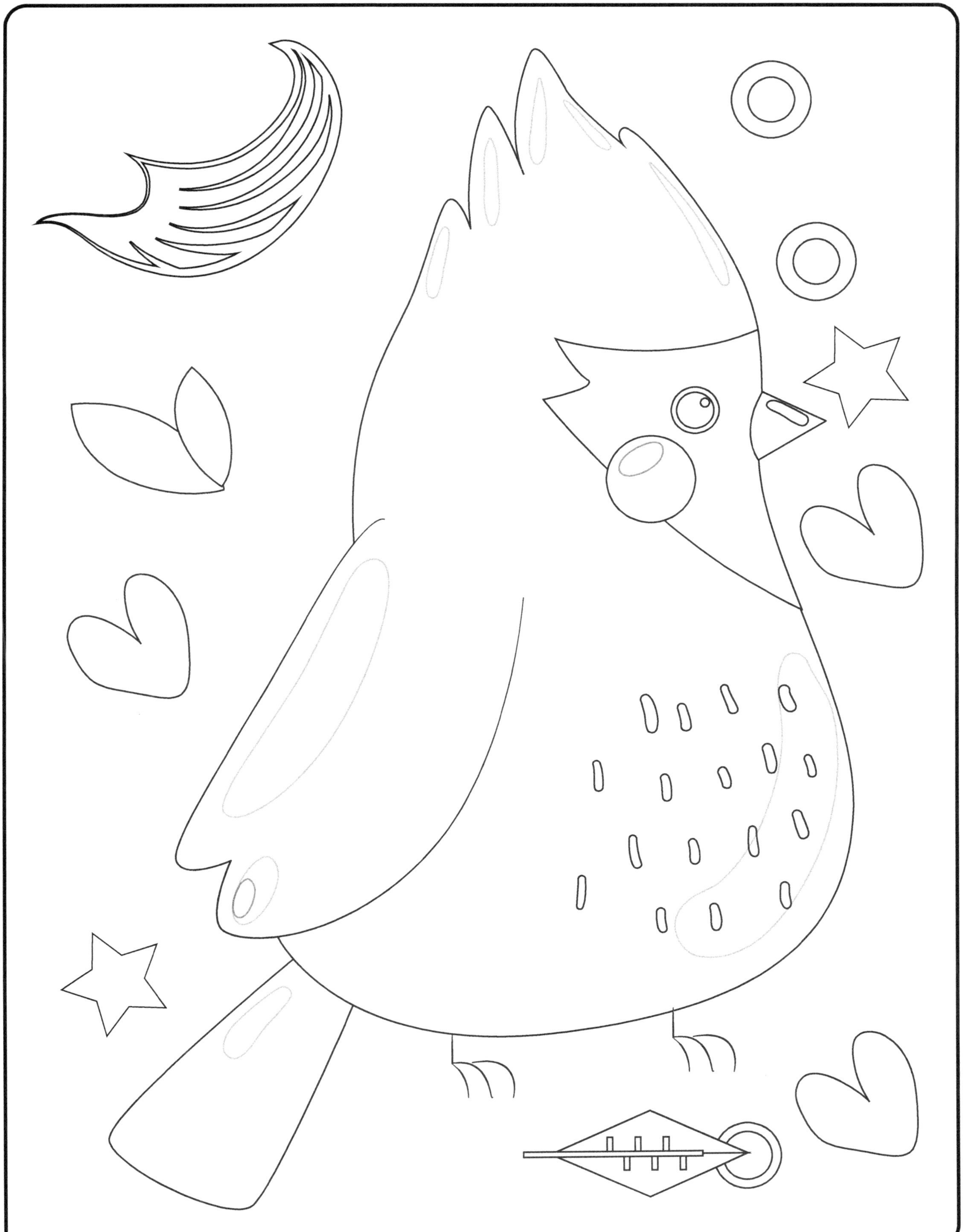

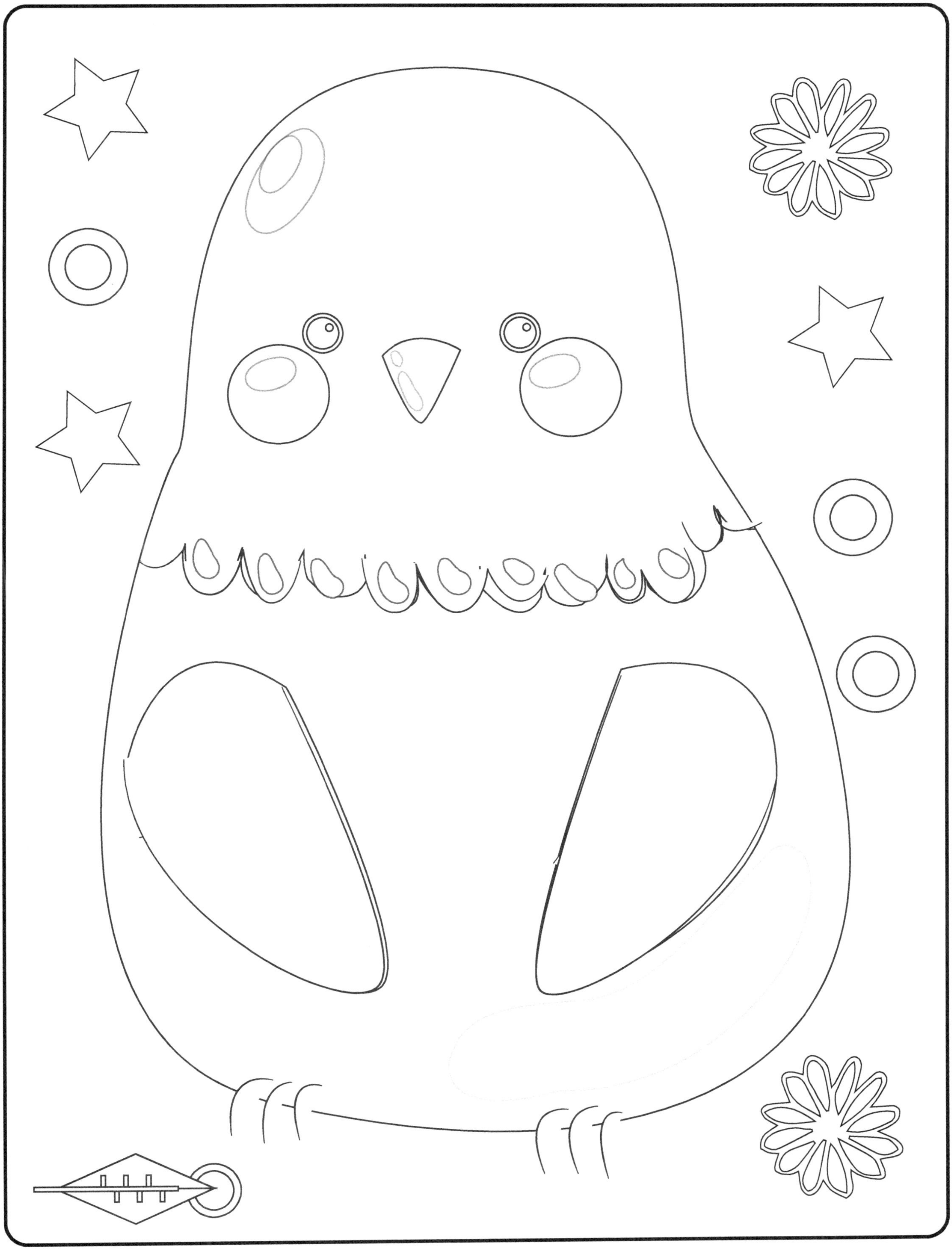

CPSIA information can be obtained
at www.ICGtesting.com
Printed in the USA
LVHW061058020621
689062LV00024B/1240

9 785936 827211